DATE DUE

apl/22/an			
4/27/AM			
4/28 AM			
4/30 AM			
DEC 1 4			
JAN 2 5 OCT 2			
MAY 2 0			
GAYLORD			PRINTED IN U.S A.

INSIDE INTERPOL

Combatting World Crime
Through Science and International Police Cooperation

MICHAEL FOONER

Coward, McCann & Geoghegan, Inc.

New York

CONTENTS

364.12
F

The pictures in this book were supplied through the courtesy of Interpol (General secretariat, and NCB's in Washington and Wiesbaden); the Drug Enforcement Administration; U.S. Secret Service; U.S. Customs Service; Jon Joosten; Wide World Photos, pp. 3 top, 35 top; UPI, pp. 22, 36, 37 top left, 44, and cover; Robert Volpe, p. 38; Fairfax County, Virginia Police Department, p. 42.

The advice and guidance during the preparation of this manuscript by Jean Nepote, Secretary-General of Interpol, David R. Macdonald, U.S. Assistant Secretary of the Treasury, and Louis B. Sims, Chief of Interpol-Washington, are greatfully acknowledged and for the selection of photographs, Steve Philips of Wide World Photos.

SBN: GB-698-30576-0
SBN: TR-698-20323-2
08 up   Library of Congress Catalog Card Number: 75-4252

That's What Interpol Is For!

One morning in August, 1970, a two-engine private airplane landed in a remote section of a Middle Eastern country, Lebanon, on an open field. The engines continued running while fifteen Lebanese men began loading sixty 100-pound sacks of hashish, a drug that is illegal in the United States.

Five American smugglers were using the airplane in what they thought was a clever scheme to bring the hashish to the United States, where they expected to sell it and make a huge profit. They had started out from San Francisco and Sacramento, California, had flown across Canada and on to Amsterdam, then zigzagged across Europe, touched down in Cyprus, then on to Lebanon.

Unknown to them, they were being tracked, by the International Criminal Police Organization—Interpol.

Coded radio messages from Interpol alerted the police of each country as the airplane progressed to its destination. When they went in for a landing, the local police patrols quietly moved in after them. The native loaders had just put thirteen sacks on board, but when the police appeared, the American smugglers closed the hatches and took off amid a hail of bullets.

The Lebanese police sent air force jets after the smugglers, but the fugitives, with an ex-U.S. Air Force pilot at the controls, got away, flying an evasive course over the Mediterranean. Interpol advised police of all countries in the area to alert their airports. Soon, on Cyprus an airport control tower received a radio request for permission to land and refuel. With Interpol monitoring the proceedings, the airplane was permitted to land, identified as the fugitive, and taken into custody.

The five American smugglers were arrested, their cargo of drugs was confiscated, and they were tried, convicted, and sentenced to prison terms. When the case was reported by news media around the world, it was described as an exciting "cops-and-robbers" story.

To the men and women of Interpol, however, it was one of many equally drama-filled events. "That's what Interpol is for," said one of its experts when a news reporter interviewed him. "It provides the machinery by which police of various countries can work together against international crime and international criminals."

In this instance, it was the United States that received assistance. The smugglers had conspired to bring 6,000 pounds of illicit drugs into the country at a huge profit to themselves. This was prevented through the voluntary cooperation of a dozen foreign countries, coordinated by Interpol. The United States has been a member of Interpol, by act of Congress, since 1938.

What Is International Crime, How Big Is It?

Interpol is a unique organization. It came into existence because criminals sometimes have a unique form of protection. Each country has laws against crimes, and people who violate those laws are considered criminals. But each law applies only within its own country. There are no international criminal laws. Since police and courts have no authority outside their own country, national frontiers became a form of protection for criminals. A person committing a crime could be immune to the consequences if he went to another country.

Many criminals make a practice of crimes spread over two or more countries, and international criminal activity has grown to very serious proportions. In the twentieth century the extraordinary expansion of travel facilities and of commerce between nations has made such growth possible.

Many lawbreakers also hope to escape detection and punishment by assuming false names and false identities, using falsified passports and documents that appear to have been issued by a foreign country. Interpol has established the means for penetrating such "disguises" and for keeping track of lawbreakers' activities and movements from country to country.

"International crime" is, technically, not a legal term, but it is a useful and handy phrase. It describes a form of criminal activity for which there would be no practical remedy were it not for Interpol.

How Interpol Began

International criminal activity expanded alarmingly at the start of this century, and it "exploded" after World War I. In 1923 a group of leading police officers, lawyers, and judges met in Vienna, Austria, to take up the challenge. They laid the foundations for police cooperation through an international criminal police organization that has since grown famous throughout the world by its code name, Interpol.

How Interpol Got Its Name

Originally it was called the International Criminal Police Commission, a name it kept for thirty-three years. After World War II newspaper reporters became interested in its activities and learned that a code name, Interpol, was used inside the organization as a telegraphic address and as an on-the-air radio signal. The press began to refer to the organization as Interpol for brevity—but then it seemed somehow glamorous, with the overtones of "foreign intrigue." One of the delegates, Dr. Giuseppe Dosi, a lively man from Italy, suggested the code name be adopted as part of the official name, and the General Assembly agreed to a change, to International Criminal Police Organization—INTERPOL. Now officials often find it necessary to make public explanations that they are not glamorous characters from a fictional television program, but that they perform real-life tasks fighting crime.

World Police Headquarters

In a quiet suburb of Paris, France, the nerve center of this organization is an austere modern building overlooking the Seine River. Here a small staff of specialists and their assistants, about 125 altogether including clerical and technical, conduct activities to ensure mutual assistance between criminal police authorities of all nations.

Interpol headquarters personnel carry no guns and make no arrests. Their job is to maintain and operate the technical machinery for police officers around the world to use in preventing crimes or bringing offenders to justice. The officials and specialists are all experienced law enforcement officers in their own country before being appointed to positions at Interpol.

They operate a central international system of criminal records and keep open the channels through which police of all nations can inform one another of progress in searching for criminals. They develop procedures for legally detaining foreign criminals—that is, offenders against laws in one country who seek refuge in another—and for shipping them back to the countries in which they committed their crimes.

Headquarters has technical units and laboratories for analyzing the vast and complex activities of the world's criminal subsocieties and for consulting with police everywhere on how best to oppose and defeat those criminal activities.

Hunting International Outlaws

The famous files of Interpol are a specially devised system of records into which are assembled the bits and pieces of information relating to an international criminal and his work. The principal purpose is to identify a suspect and his or her criminal associates quickly and to pursue them efficiently.

Information streams in from all over the world—investigation reports, photographs, fingerprints, expert testimony—more than 1,000 items a day, in a variety of languages. These items have to be analyzed immediately, sorted, and associated with what is already on file.

The rotary index shown above is one of Interpol's most vital instruments. The wheels, on the left, contain about 2,000,000 cards with names, aliases, and nicknames. The cards are classified both alphabetically and phonetically, to guard against errors owing to spelling or language variations. Even Chinese can be handled in the same filing system. On the right in this picture, Interpol staff members are matching new and old information and verifying facts that are being exchanged among outlaw hunters in various parts of the world.

The index is a "universal language" key for entering and finding one's way among world crime records. It enables detectives in Britain and Brazil, the United States and Uganda, Japan, Jordan and Israel—regardless of language differences—to assist one another. Each rotary index card is cross-referenced to folders in the detailed criminal files that hold the information for carrying out a criminal investigation, as shown in the picture below.

Keeping Track of Dangerous International Criminals

Fingerprint files and photographs (also known as mug shots or rogues' gallery) are the bones and ligaments of a criminal identification system. Interpol's, above, have to be specialized. Interpol collects fingerprints and photographs only of people known to be engaged in international offenses. Fingerprints are one of the basic tools of international criminal identification. About 100 years ago a British civil servant in India and a Scottish doctor in Japan independently discovered that no two human beings have the same skin patterns on their fingertips. Now almost every country has a fingerprint file on its own criminals.

Interpol itself does no fingerprinting. Each member country sends to Interpol duplicate sets of prints from its own files, identifying suspects believed to be internationally active. Interpol has about 130,000 ten-finger sets in its files, and about 5,000 single-print cards.

The photograph file, above right, is also very specialized, for use by police in hunting criminals who roam without leaving fingerprints. Interpol keeps photographs of about 6,000 individuals in this file, classified in a special way it has devised. The teeming waterways of Hong Kong, center right, and the sophisticated city of Marseilles, lower right, are among the many thousands of places in which international outlaws try to disappear from police attention.

Maintaining Records of the Worldwide Underworld

Interpol's criminal records were destroyed during World War II. They represented twenty years of work and were a serious loss, but after the war Interpol set about putting together a new set of records and, at the same time, adapting the system to new conditions.

The new Criminal Records Department is shown here. Its essential purposes are: (1) to compile information on criminals and their offenses and (2) to identify offenders and their MO's—so called *modus operandi*, their methods of committing crimes. Here information is collected on international criminals' passports, guns, cars, boats, and other such items. Interpol has about 500,000 such pieces of information, arranged under 125 headings. There are also records of crimes classified by type, time, and location. The object of all this is to be able to identify criminals with their offenses, regardless of how often they change names or where they go, and to trace connections between different cases in which the same individuals are involved or which have occurred separately over a period of time. These are card files—about 300,000 of them—cross-indexed to case folders, to individual dossiers, and to running records of police activity on cases that move from country to country.

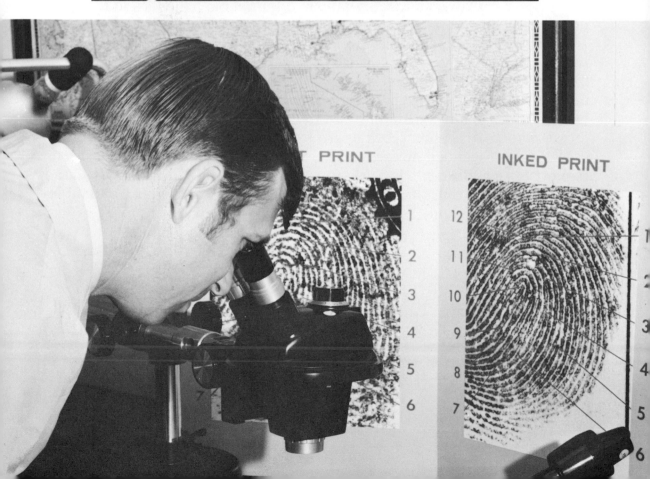

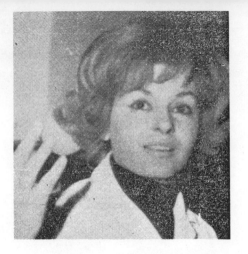

Tracing Lawbreakers Across Oceans and Continents

The work of the Criminal Records Department is available to police of member countries for their investigations or to assist them in making arrests and bringing an offender to court. In addition, Interpol has its own groups of police specialists who examine and analyze crime trends and criminal organizations throughout the world. As certain offenses become widespread—drug traffic, bank fraud, swindling, art thefts, counterfeiting, securities theft, and so on—they probe and collate information from all sources to get an overview of significant criminal movements and to advise police agencies on otherwise obscure activities of key offenders.

This woman, a persistent offender, eluded arrest for many years. She was a member of a gang that swindled banks in a score of countries halfway around the globe. She became the subject of Interpol warning notices to police forces everywhere. Newspaper pictures, above, hardly do justice to her beauty, which for a time was one of her assets in escaping arrest. The police photos below are from various stages of her criminal career. The "wanted notice," right, was circulated by Interpol at the request of several countries, asking that she be detained wherever found and returned to those countries for prosecution. Information is double-checked, lower right, before being circulated in warning and wanted notices.

HÖGEROVA

Anna.

née le 7 Mars 1937 à Prague-Nove Mesto, TCHECOSLOVAQUIE
fille de NEMECEK Antonin et de STIPKOVÁ Eva
célibataire
PROFESSION : se dit institutrice
NATIONALITÉ : indéterminée
ETAT CIVIL CONTROLE EXACT
alias : NAMATCHI Jeannette née en 1937 à Budapest.-- DE POLANSKY-CARON née le 7/3/1937 à Budapest.--
POLONSKY-CARON.-- POLANSKY-STIBEK Jeannette.-- POLANSKA Jeannette.-- ALVES-RODRIGUEZ (ou
RODRIGAS) Francisca née le 4/1/1940 à Nova Ignaçu.-- ESTERUTZ von GALANTA Alexandra.--
WEIL Elizabeth.-- KIEFFER Ingrid.-- DRAGO Rosanna.-- DUPONT Dolores née le 7/3/1937 à
Montevideo.-- KIEFER Ingrid.-- DORSEY Charlotte.-- BOURDIER Jeanne née le 19/7/1936.-- TONS
Petra née le 7/7/1937 à Paris.-- VON HOEGER Anna née le 7/3/1937 à Prague.-- SOLINAS (ou
SALINAS) D.-- Dite "Sandra".
DESCRIPTION : voir photo et empreintes digitales, taille 1 m.70, cheveux auburn, yeux marron.--
Est atteinte d'une légère claudication. Corpulence svelte, teint clair. Porte de temps en
temps une perruque - se teint les cheveux. Parle français, anglais, allemand, espagnol,
portugais et tchèque.

MAIN DROITE					RIGHT HAND
POUCE / THUMB	INDEX / FORE FINGER	MEDIUS / MIDDLE FINGER	ANNULAIRE / RING FINGER	AURICULAIRE / LITTLE FINGER	
MAIN GAUCHE					LEFT HAND

DACTYLOSCOPIEE ET PHOTOGRAPHIEE A LUCERNE, SUISSE, le 12/10/1968

RENSEIGNEMENTS :
Signalée au BRESIL en 1963 pour usage de fausse identité. Recherchée en ALLEMAGNE FEDERALE, à la demande du Tribunal de Heidelberg en date du 14/5/1964 pour escroquerie au chèque sans provisions. A fait l'objet de la notice internationale de recherche n°681/64 A 5270 annulée par avis de cessation de recherche (voir liste n°201 d'avril 1966). Signalée à Rotterdam, PAYS BAS, pour émission de faux chèques (le 9/9/1964). Arrêtée le 17/10/1964 à Beyrouth, LIBAN, pour émission de faux chèques, remise en liberté sous caution le 6/2/1965, s'est enfuie du LIBAN. Arrêtée à Milan, ITALIE, le 28/4/1965 pour escroquerie aux faux chèques et remise en liberté provisoire le 29/12/1965. Arrêtée à Lucerne, SUISSE, le 12/10/1968 pour émission de faux chèques.---- Complices : ROMAN SZUMAN Ricardo (notice internationale n°270/64 A 5456).- COCUCCI Oswaldo (notice internationale n°369/64 A 5269).- MEROLLA Franco, né le 14/10/1933 à Rome. Arrêté en ITALIE le 10/10/1968.----
A utilisé, entre autres, les pièces d'identité suivantes (falsifiées) : passeport autrichien n°140.231 délivré à COSTA RICA; passeport portugais n°3684 délivré au nom de DORSEY Charlotte; passeport italien n°3686655 délivré au nom de MAIMINALLI Violetta le 15/7/1965 par le Consulat d'ITALIE au Havre, FRANCE. (En réalité il s'agit du passeport n°3 626675/546 délivré à Gelmi.prénom Violetta); passeport péruvien n°128131 délivré au nom de WEIL Elisabeth le 20/6/1964; passeport péruvien n°128129 délivré au nom de DRAGO Rosanna, le 8/3/1964; permis de conduire italien n°613 214 A 008 délivré à Trieste au nom de TONS Petra née le 7/7/1937.---- Individu ayant tendance à commettre plus spécialement des escroqueries au chèque ou au traveller chèque falsifié.

MOTIF DE LA DIFFUSION :
Malfaiteur. Marque une tendance à commettre des délits sur le plan international. Il est conseillé de surveiller ses activités s'il séjourne dans votre pays. En cas de nouvelle infraction, prière d'aviser l'O.I.P.C.-INTERPOL, Secrétariat Général, 26 rue Armengaud, 92 St.Cloud (INTERPOL PARIS).

O.I.P.C. PARIS
Janvier 1969

N° du dossier :
N° de contrôle :

Catching High-flying
Crooks Red-handed

The climax of a criminal investigation is shown here. Police of several countries cooperated in penetrating a gold-smuggling conspiracy. Above, the gang's resident contact is waiting at the airport. Above right, he is meeting the courier. Center left, they are getting ready to move through the customs barrier, but police have been alerted that the traveling courier has, under his shirt, a vest packed with gold bars, center right. Below, police agents have moved in, have taken him into custody, and have confiscated the smuggled gold.

14

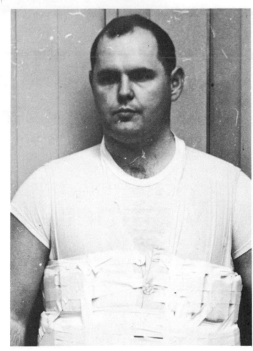

Member Countries

Interpol is the world's oldest existing organization of international cooperation. It is governed by its General Assembly, above, consisting of delegates from all member countries, under its own constitution. Although each member country designates the police agency to represent it, Interpol maintains independence from the countries themselves. The headquarters is officially called the General Secretariat, and Interpol contact units, called National Central Bureaus, are set up in each member country.

The president of Interpol is elected every four years. There is an Executive Committee, consisting of three vice-presidents and nine delegates in addition to the president. All operations are carried on at the General Secretariat by a staff of about 125, headed by the secretary-general, who is the chief full-time official of the organization. He is appointed by the General Assembly for a period of five years.

Every year, usually in September or October, the General Assembly meets for about a week in a different city in a different part of the world. It discusses, plans and decides on major matters of international crime, on prevention and countermeasures.

Its budget is about $2,000,000 annually. The money comes from annual dues paid by each member country on a scale reflecting its relative wealth and standard of living.

President of Interpol
William L. Higgitt
Former Commissioner of the
Royal Canadian Mounted Police

Secretary-General of Interpol
Jean Nepote

U.S. Representative to Interpol
David R. Macdonald
Assistant Secretary of Treasury

Member of Executive Committee
For the Americas
H. Stuart Knight

MEMBER COUNTRIES

AFRICA
Algeria
Burundi
Cameroon
Central African
   Republic
Chad
Congo
Dahomey
Egyptian Arab
   Republic
Ethiopia
Gabon
Ghana
Guinea
Ivory Coast
Kenya
Lesotho
Liberia
Libya
Madagascar
Malawi
Mali
Mauritania
Mauritius
Morocco
Niger
Nigeria
Quatar
Rwanda
Senegal
Sierra Leone
Sudan
Tanzania
Togo
Tunisia
Uganda
Upper Volta
Zaire
Zambia

THE AMERICAS
Argentina
Bolivia
Brazil
Canada
Chile
Colombia
Costa Rica
Cuba
Dominican Republic
Ecuador
El Salvador
Guatemala
Guyana
Haiti
Honduras
Jamaica
Mexico
Netherlands Antilles
Nicaragua
Panama
Peru
Surinam
Trinidad and Tobago
United States of America
Uruguay
Venezuela

ASIA/OCEANIA
Australia
Bahrain
Burma
China (Republic of)
Cyprus
Fiji
India
Indonesia
Iran
Iraq
Israel
Japan
Jordan
Khmer Republic
Korea
Kuwait
Laos
Lebanon
Malaysia
Nauru
Nepal
New Zealand
Oman
Pakistan
Philippines
Saudi Arabia
Singapore
Sri Lanka
Syria
Thailand
United Arab Emirates
Vietnam

EUROPE
Austria
Belgium
Denmark
Federal German Republic
Finland
France
Greece
Iceland
Ireland
Italy
Liechtenstein
Luxembourg
Malta
Monaco
Netherlands
Norway
Portugal
Rumania
Spain
Sweden
Switzerland
Turkey
United Kingdom of Great
   Britain and Northern Ireland
Yugoslavia

Operating a Global Communications Network

Fast and reliable communications are the lifeblood of any crime-fighting organization; for international operations, such a system is crucial. Interpol members use international telephones, cables, teletype systems, even the Telstar service, but they also have to have an independent set of global facilities that are confidential and exclusive to police work.

Interpol established a radio network to meet this need, supplementing it with a phototelegraphic system for exchange of pictures and fingerprints and a radio teleprinter system that automatically types out broadcast messages. Above right is the radio operations room at headquarters and at center is the remote control tie with sixteen transmitters operated from headquarters. Below can be seen the fifty-foot aerial rising from the headquarters roof. About eighty miles south of France are the great towers emitting the signals that flash around the globe: "Radio Interpol Calling!"

Radio Network

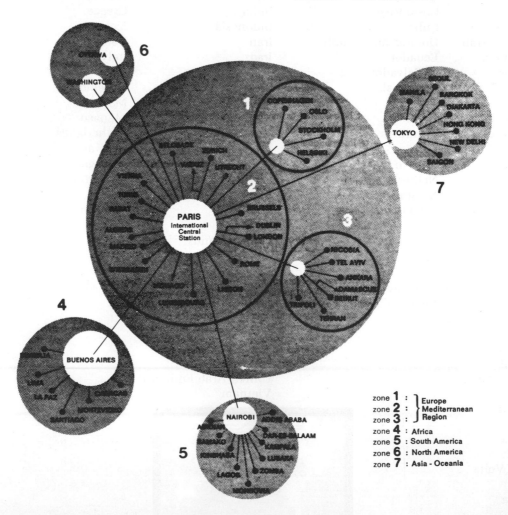

zone **1** : ⎫
zone **2** : ⎬ Europe Mediterranean Region
zone **3** : ⎭
zone **4** : Africa
zone **5** : South America
zone **6** : North America
zone **7** : Asia - Oceania

The USA, One of the Most Active Members

The United States' Bureau of Interpol is located in Washington, D.C., with offices, above, in the Treasury Building, across the street from the White House. It is linked to the worldwide police network by radio, teletype, telephone, and cable, above right. More than 1,000 requests a year come in from federal, state, city, and county police officers for foreign investigations of persons violating American local, state, or federal criminal laws, and the American Interpol Bureau directs the request to the foreign Interpol Bureau concerned. At the same time, more than 2,800 requests come in from around the world, from foreign police needing assistance with their criminal investigations inside the United States.

When an American police officer needs foreign assistance it can be an APB, a request that will circle the globe, or a regional request to a certain few countries, or a request to one foreign country. In one instance, a Maryland widow had a valuable diamond stolen; the thief was caught, but he had sent the diamond to a friend in Hong Kong; at the Maryland sheriff's request, the Interpol Bureau in Washington requested aid from the Hong Kong police, and soon the widow's diamond was on its way back to her. In another case, a California woman disappeared while on a business trip through Europe; the Los Angeles district attorney, through Interpol, gained the cooperation of police in a dozen European countries in searching for her; they discovered she was the victim of foul play, and they helped bring the murderer to justice in California.

The chief of the American Bureau of Interpol and his two assistants are shown in conference above. Each year the United States sends a delegation of leading police officials to attend the General Assembly, below right, to work with other countries on major problems of drug traffic, skyjacking, theft of art masterpieces, stock fraud, counterfeiting, criminal violence, smuggling, and other crimes that have become more threatening all over the world. This is how they pave the way for cooperation.

Police of All Nations
Linked as a Team

The real-life fight against world crime is never carried on by superdetectives or by any international squad. It never has and probably never will be. Each country is responsible for its own law enforcement, in its own territory, through its own police. Each member nation wants it that way. The real-life effort to stamp out crime does, however, involve concerted action and mutual assistance by police of various countries. Interpol makes this possible, providing the mechanisms that, when needed, can link camel-riding cops of an African desert nation with highly sophisticated police of an industrially advanced nation. Facilities vary, but each country contributes what it can. The camel police, above, with their intimate knowledge of African desert terrain, contrast dramatically with the highly technological organization of the West German police, below right. This complex of buildings was designed specially for the National Central Bureau of Interpol in West Germany. Each member country has its own form of Interpol bureau to serve as link with all other nations' bureaus.

The Struggle to Control Dangerous Drugs

One of the oldest examples of international police cooperation is that concerned with control of illicit traffic in narcotics. Such traffic is complicated and far-reaching; flowers grown in the East are harvested for opium, which, after complicated travels and conversions into heroin, enters black markets in cities of distant continents. Soon after Interpol was organized, member countries agreed it should work on this problem and in 1926 it took its first steps. To start with, interchange of information was needed. Gradually this evolved into a central records system for identifying the drug traffickers, their methods, and their gangs, tracing their operations, secret laboratories, and smuggling routes. Above is a secret heroin laboratory in the south of France, next to it is a cargo of hides shipped into a Pacific Ocean port with concealed packages of heroin, and above right are native dealers in Southeast Asia making a shipment of heroin ready for a clandestine voyage they hope will carry it to the black market of Hong Kong, Japan, or the United States. Freighters like this one, center right, play an important part in the illicit world traffic in drugs, as do airplanes, trucks, automobiles, and every other conceivable conveyance.

Below right, law enforcement inspectors have uncovered an illegal freighter shipment of drugs. Interpol also works closely with international health organizations and with the United Nations Commission on Narcotic Drugs, the Council of Europe, the Conference of South American Countries, and the Conference of Southeast Asia Countries.

Breaking the "French Connection"

Through Interpol and its specialists, police of all countries exchange information about the new and old methods used by drug smugglers. Criminals repeat a maneuver that succeeds and copy from one another. One notorious method was to conceal heroin in spaces and special compartments in exported automobiles. Law enforcement officials have learned how to detect these schemes by probing and dismantling the hiding places. It became the subject of a popular American motion picture called *The French Connection*, which was based on an actual case of attempted heroin smuggling from France. These photographs show similar instances of discovering drugs concealed in imported automobiles. Such seizures follow exchanges of information through Interpol facilities.

26

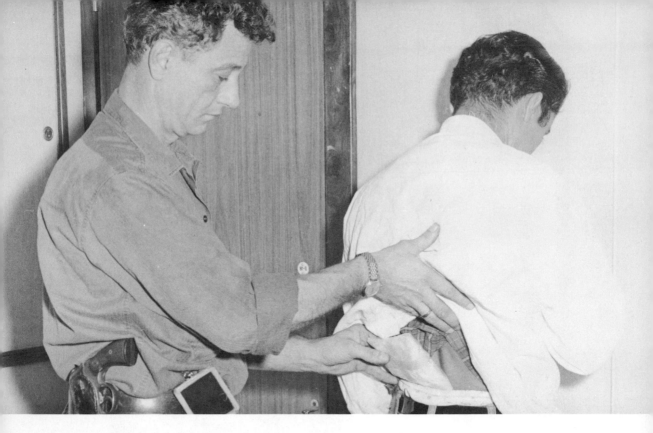

False Bottoms, False Pregnancies

The devices and schemes of smugglers go on and on, ranging from ingenious to simple—or simple-minded. Training law enforcement officers to detect these schemes has become one of the very important elements in the worldwide efforts to control dangerous drugs, and Interpol has an important role in this. It arranges for scientifically advanced police to train officers of countries that don't have their own training facilities. It also assembles training materials for distribution to assist all nations in working together.

These kinds of activity supplement the day-to-day operations of circulating information about movements of known traffickers and routes of shipments and for coordination in police raids and arrests.

Above, a body-carrying drug courier is being arrested; next is shown an ingenious contrivance by which a woman drug courier pretends she is pregnant to bring more than eight pounds of narcotics to the black market. Upper right, the courier has many pounds of drugs taped and bandaged to his body under his clothing, but law enforcement officers are trained to detect these tricks. They have also learned to find contraband in compartments of false-bottom luggage and shoes, in hollowed-out objects of all sorts, and in thousands of places of attempted concealment.

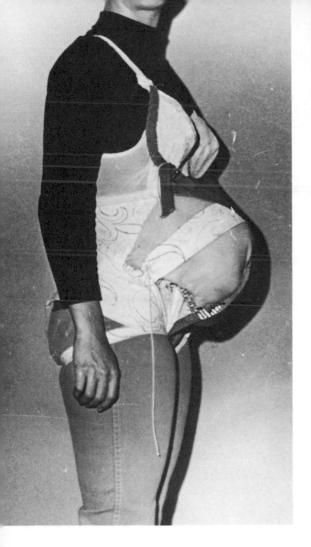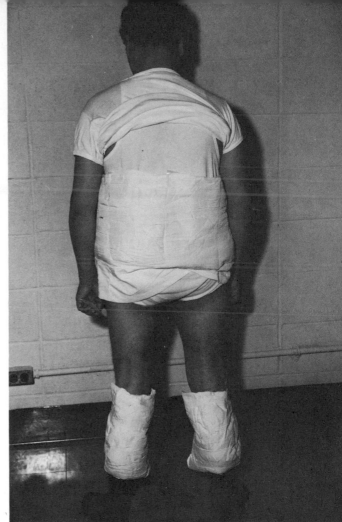

Taking the Profit Out of Smuggling

Everyone loves a bargain, and the public is often complacent about smuggling since it may lead to purchases at bargain prices. But smugglers and smuggling gangs are often closely linked to other types of crime such as theft, counterfeiting, bribery, drug traffic, and murder. Worldwide smuggling of gold and diamonds, works of art, industrial components and manufactured goods, luxuries, and even human beings, adds up to an enormous amount of illegal activity that is difficult to stop. At one time smuggling was considered a separate problem for each nation's customs authorities, but in modern times smuggling conspiracies are actually large-scale criminal operations reaching into the underworld of several nations. Police in all parts of the world have found it necessary to turn to Interpol for help against smugglers and their related criminal offenses. Interpol's centralized records for identifying leaders and gangs, and its channels for police cooperation, provide assistance in arrests and in seizures of articles such as liquor, jewelry, import specialties, and gold coins, as shown in these photographs, as well as automobiles, expensive machines, cigarettes, and almost anything of commercial value.

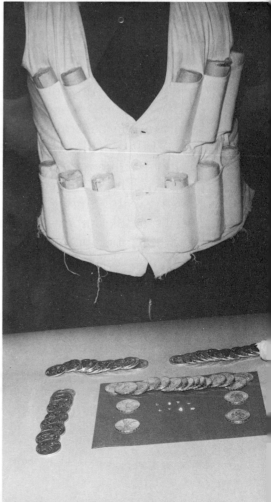

"Funny Money"
Is No Laughing Matter

Bogus money is as old as money itself, but in modern times counterfeit currency and coins have become vast enterprises involving many millions of dollars annually. Currencies of nearly all nations are subject to counterfeiting; but some are more popular with counterfeiters than others, and American dollars are the most popular of all, especially in foreign countries. Very often, counterfeits of one country are circulated in several other countries. One "famous" printing of counterfeit dollars originally made in 1946 has been found circulating in thirty-three countries and was still in circulation more than twenty-five years after being printed.

Counterfeiting continues to be a serious international crime. It was one of the earliest to become a special responsibility of Interpol. Today its laboratories, central indexes, and training operations are essential to the functioning of the world's monetary systems.

Its involvement began in 1929 with a mandate from the League of Nations. The technical center at Interpol Headquarters is considered the world's watchdog against money that is not genuine. Seizures of counterfeiter's stocks, above, often require complex investigations. At Interpol headquarters, above right, examples of every genuine and every counterfeit issue of currency are maintained for reference and for purpose of investigations.

More than 6,000 types of counterfeits have been classified at the headquarters laboratory, imitations of the currency of eighty-nine countries. More than 235 types of checks and traveler's checks imitating those issued by banks in twenty-two countries have also been studied.

But counterfeiters do not live by money alone. Corporate stocks and bonds and government securities are also prime subjects, below right, as well as credit cards, money orders, and airline tickets.

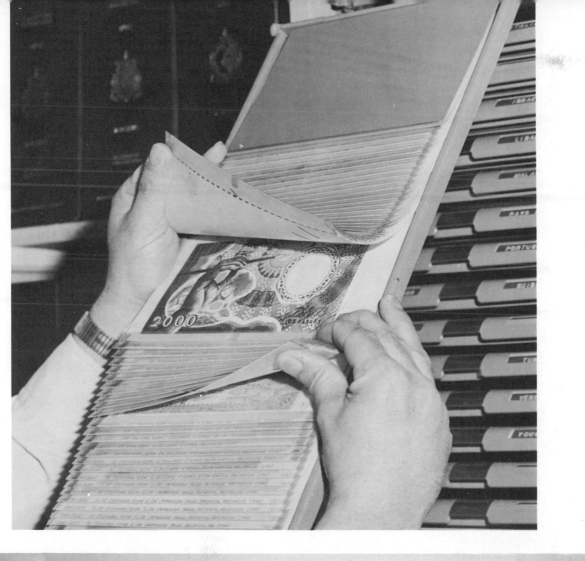

Forgers Lurk Everywhere

Check forgery, fraud, and swindling business schemes are a growing form of criminal activity. International swindlers travel a great deal, are well informed, speak several languages, and are often imaginative, as well as personable. They cross national frontiers as business travelers or as tourists, quite openly, even when traveling under assumed identities.

Interpol's files often provide the only means for catching up with them, through the pooling and exchanging of police information from different countries where they have worked.

Above, an expert is analyzing forgers' handwritings and signatures. Often police analysis has to be highly technical and sophisticated and has to be transmitted rapidly to interrupt a scheme or to apprehend a swindler and his accomplices before their well-planned flight. Interpol headquarters has a specialist unit concentrating on these types of offenses.

Fighting Traffic in Human Beings

The picture above shows slave children who were forced to work in a Bangkok factory under inhuman conditions until police raided the factory and set them free. Despite worldwide disapproval and laws everywhere against it, human beings are still bought and sold.

Twenty years before Interpol came into existence there was an international Convention Against Slave Traffic, but slavery has never been completely wiped out. Nearly fifty years later, in 1951, another international agreement, the Convention for Suppression of Traffic in Persons and of the Exploitation of Prostitution, was brought into force. Interpol machinery has been used on many occasions against people who engage in obtaining, transporting, and exploiting humans. These cases frequently involve young women who are fooled into going to foreign countries to work as "entertainers," "dancers," "hostesses," and the like—they are then forced to work as prostitutes. Interpol has conducted surveys in present-day practices of slavery, and in 1972 it furnished a report to the Human Rights Division of the United Nations. On a continuing basis, Interpol collaborates with the Economic and Social Council of the United Nations for reporting and suppressing slavery.

Combating Terror

One day in September, 1972, the Interpol Bureau of Lebanon, located in Beirut, radioed the Interpol Bureau in Nicosia on Cyprus. They warned that there was a time bomb on board an airliner then flying over the Mediterranean, bound for Rome, with 102 persons on board. Interpol-Nicosia intercepted the pilot and brought him in for an emergency landing, whereupon the local police searched the aircraft and found the bomb which was set to go off a short time later. They removed it, and 102 lives were saved. Another incident, above, did not end so fortunately.

Interpol was one of the first organizations to realize that the wave of airplane hijacking, bombing and kidnapping that began shortly after World War II was a serious new form of worldwide crime. Ordinary police action, such as the one that saved the aircraft over Cyprus, is not enough to handle the whole problem. Interpol experts began a series of special studies: of airplane crimes, in 1954; bomb hoaxes, in 1967; hijackings, in 1969; anonymous phone calls, in 1970. After each study, it proposed various types of security measures for the protection of aircraft and people, in the air and on the ground. Working with other international bodies, Interpol developed joint action programs for all nations. Practical systems have been devised and disseminated by Interpol for cooperation between police and airline personnel in each country to prevent violent crimes by terrorists. Interpol circulates warning information and preventive methods. Above, such a warning is posted for public safety. Above right is a collection of seized firearms carried illegally across a national frontier; below right, postal employees inspect letters to intercept those which may be carrying bombs.

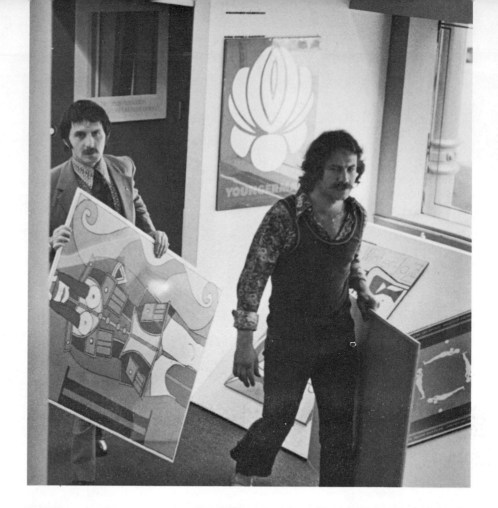

Protecting Cultural Heritage

A grave upsurge of thefts of art objects has developed around the world. Museums, churches, and private collections are being looted more and more. Archaeological sites with cultural treasures are also being extensively pillaged.

Just as Interpol circulates wanted notices on criminals, it circulates wanted notices on stolen art objects. These notices, above right, become useful when valuable items are discovered far from home in suspicious circumstances. Detectives in local police forces are able to conduct prompt investigations, as shown above, to determine whether suspected items have in fact been stolen. It then becomes possible to arrange for owners—private collectors and institutions—to make recovery. Shown below is an example of the recovery of a valuable picture painted by the famous French artist Maurice Utrillo.

At headquarters, Interpol has set up an index of stolen artworks, which enables the tracing of the origins of a work suspected of being stolen. It also devises methods that museums can use to prevent thefts from taking place.

LES 12 OEUVRES D'ART   THE 12 MOST WANTED WORKS OF ART

Notice publiée par l'O.I.P.C. - INTERPOL   Published by the I.C.P.O. - INTERPOL   26 Rue Armengaud, 92210 Saint Cloud (France)

En cas de découverte ou de renseignements   If found or anything be known of these cases, please contact the police who will inform their Interpol NCB.
de police qui informeront leur Bureau Central

N° 3 - JUNE 1973

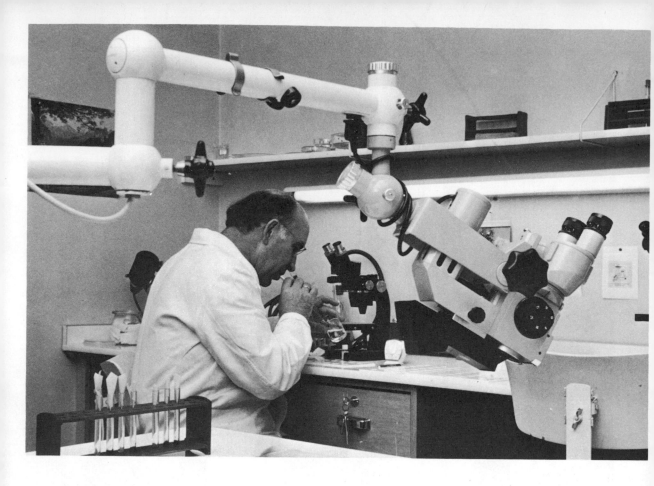

Enlisting Science

   Scientific police work, called forensic science, began to take on major importance in the nineteenth century. Today in police laboratories all over the world scientific procedures are applied in the examination of physical evidence to obtain proof of crimes and detect offenders. But there is a special problem: that of communication among the scientists and police organizations who develop and test advanced techniques. Interpol provides channels through which such knowledge may be exchanged and shared. Of all the technical procedures, fingerprint identification is probably best known to the public, but most branches of science, including atomic science, also play their parts. Electronic identification of voices, chemical analysis of drugs to trace their geographical origins, advanced methods for determining causes of death are among the subjects discussed. Interpol organizes and conducts meetings, or symposia, at which experts from various countries can meet and exchange knowledge and also decide on programs of research which should be pursued at the various laboratories. Shown here are laboratories of Interpol national bureaus in Europe. Interpol headquarters also publishes some scientific papers and compiles reference sources for dissemination to scientists.

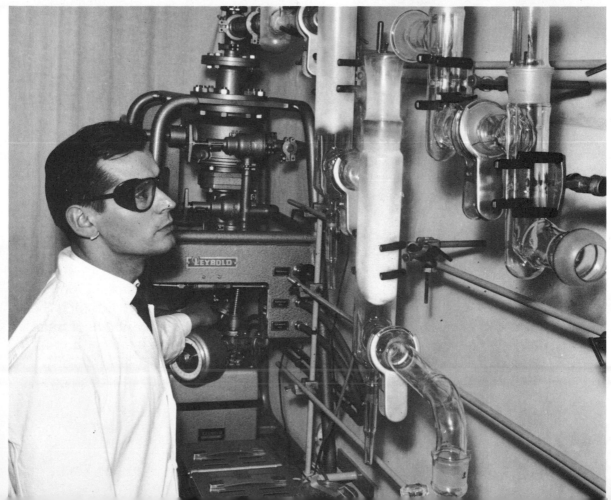

"Man's Best Friend" Detects Lawbreakers

Dogs have entered the international crime scene in recent years. Historically, dogs have been used to guard people and property. They later became known for their ability in hunting fugitives and prison escapers. More recently, with the vast pressure from illicit narcotics traffic on police resources, it was found feasible to use dogs for detecting concealed drugs. As traffickers began to send contraband narcotics through the mails, dogs were brought into post offices, right, and put to work sniffing out suspicious packages. When attacks against international airlines came along, it was determined that dogs' sense of smell could be used to detect the presence of explosives, pictured above. Interpol has developed technical studies on the use of dogs for distribution to all nations plagued with these problems. With training, dog-and-handler teams can protect aircraft, office buildings, and utilities against bombings and can detect both drugs and explosives sent through the international mails.

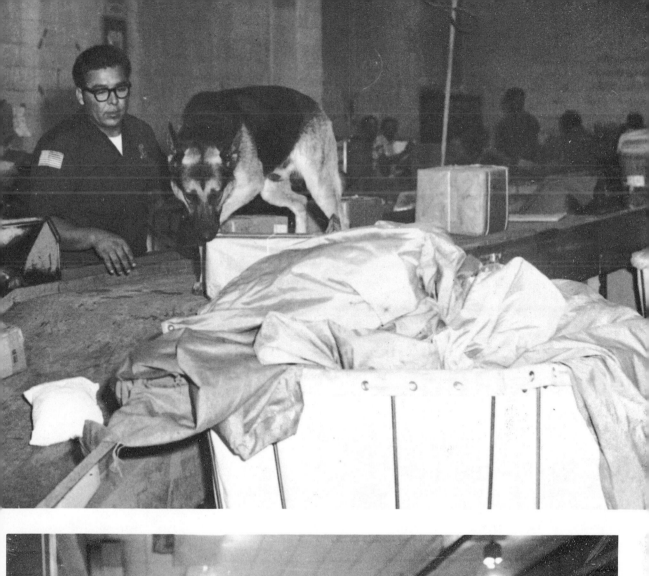

Patrolling the World's Skyways, Highways, and Seaways

Flight from the scene of the crime is the offender's first line of defense. Crimes such as drug trafficking, smuggling, and arms traffic are not the only ones in which offenders escape by getting out of the country. One gang of male burglars set up their headquarters in Italy, where they carefully refrained from any crimes whatsoever, systematically traveling to Belgium, Germany, France, Luxembourg, and Switzerland to commit more than 100 burglaries and armed robberies. Women accomplices went ahead of them to carry out surveillances of their targets, act as lookouts, and transport their guns. It took the combined work of police in all those countries to disband this gang.

Interpol's facilities for coordinating police countermeasures make it possible to guard against movements of criminals by land, sea and air. Above, a team of police specialists are bringing to light plastic sacks of contraband that were attached to the hull of an ocean freighter below the waterline. Above right, a team of special motorcycle police are making a fast run to intercept offenders attempting to cross the frontier in automobiles. Below right, a team of helicopter-borne police have tracked a courier attempting to slip across the frontier where it stretches through the open countryside. Members of Interpol receive the benefit of advance information on criminal activities such as these.

International Criminals Brought to Justice

For success in fighting world crime, there have to be quick exchanges of information, methods for prompt arrests, and effective procedures for bringing offenders to the country where they committed their crimes to be tried. The last of these three items can be the most complicated and difficult. Taking a person from one country to another is not a police matter. It is a matter involving the sovereignty of nations, where police interests are subordinate to their country's diplomatic and foreign affairs authorities. However, it usually takes a long time to get something done through diplomatic channels, and that creates opportunity for a criminal to escape. To overcome this problem, Interpol has developed model treaties and laws to speed up action on wanted criminals and fugitives. These are gradually being adopted by member nations. In many countries now, an Interpol wanted notice is recognized as a legal basis for arrest. Police can then move quickly and lawfully to detain the person while the machinery of extradition gets into motion. In some cases extradition treaties between countries do not exist or do not apply to a case in hand. Then cooperation may take another form, such as expelling the criminal or refusing him admission, so that the country where he is wanted for prosecution can catch up with him.

Above, Auguste Ricord, one of the largest smugglers of heroin in South America, is shown en route to stand trial in New York after evading extradition for a year. Above right, Adolfo Sobocki-Tobias, accused of heading a huge narcotics-smuggling ring, is brought to the United States for prosecution after having been expelled by the government of Chile. Below right, members of an international ring, after coordinated raids in several locations, are being escorted to a lockup.

46

Blairsville High School Library

Concern for Human Rights

This group of police specialists is meeting to handle a crime problem that stretches across the oceans, from North and South America to Europe and the Far East.

High-speed transportation and super high-speed communications developed by the lawful members of society are also used by the unlawful for greed and violence. Because this enables criminals to disregard geographical boundaries, crime fighting requires that international cooperation become highly developed.

Interpol was conceived to serve the needs of the international community while carefully refraining from encroaching on any nation's internal affairs. Thus, it has been able to function effectively in a world where cultures are vastly different.

By its constitution it is concerned only with "common" crimes and prohibits any concern with racial, religious, political, or military matters. Its program includes problems concerned with protection of freedom in the practices of criminal justice. It is specifically—by its constitution—dedicated to the principles of the Universal Declaration of Human Rights and is the only police organization in the world officially declaring itself in this way.